POLICE TALK

A SCENARIO-BASED COMMUNICATIONS WORKBOOK FOR POLICE RECRUITS AND OFFICERS

JEAN REYNOLDS Ph.D.
MAJOR MARY MARIANI Ph.D.

DEBBIE J. GOODMAN
Series Editor

Upper Saddle River, New Jersey 07458

Library of Congress Cataloging-in-Publication Data

Reynolds, Jean
    Police talk : a scenario-based communications workbook for police
    recruits and officers
    / Jean Reynolds, Mary Mariani.
        p. cm.— (P.A.C.T.)
    ISBN 0-13-089588-1 (alk. paper)
    1. Communication in law enforcement. 2. Police-community
    relations. I. Mariani,
    Mary. II. Title. III. P.A.C.T. (Upper Saddle River, NJ)

HV7936.C79 R49 2002
363.2'01'4—dc21

00-064327

Publisher: Jeff Johnston
Senior Acquisitions Editor: Kim Davies
Production Editor: Janet Kiefer, Carlisle Publishers Services
Production Liaison: Barbara Marttine Cappuccio
Director of Production and Manufacturing: Bruce Johnson
Managing Editor: Mary Carnis
Manufacturing Buyer: Cathleen Petersen
Art Director: Marianne Frasco
Cover Design Coordinator: Miguel Ortiz
Cover Photo: © Tracey Williams/Courtesy of the Somerset County (NJ) Police
    Academy, Deputy Chief Richard Celeste, Training Director
Cover Design: Bruce Kenselaar
Marketing Manager: Ramona Sherman
Editorial Assistant: Sarah Holle
Interior Design and Composition: Carlisle Communications, Ltd.

Prentice-Hall International (UK) Limited, *London*
Prentice-Hall of Australia Pty. Limited, *Sydney*
Prentice-Hall Canada Inc., *Toronto*
Prentice-Hall Hispanoamericana, S.A., *Mexico*
Prentice-Hall of India Private Limited, *New Delhi*
Prentice-Hall of Japan, Inc., *Tokyo*
Prentice-Hall Singapore Pte. Ltd.
Editora Prentice-Hall do Brasil, Ltda., *Rio de Janeiro*

ISBN 0-13-089588-1

To Sandy Hall and the Thornhill family,

especially Mella and Doug, for their encouragement

and support through the years

CONTENTS

PREFACE

Communication skills save lives. *Police Talk* was written to help both recruits and experienced officers develop and sharpen the verbal skills so important to modern police work.

As law enforcement becomes more complex and sophisticated, communication is more important than ever before. Police officers need expertise in conflict resolution, assertiveness, use of authority, interviewing, and a host of other skills. Today's emphasis on community policing challenges officers to protect public safety while showing sensitivity to victims and citizens with special needs. Domestic violence, another area receiving intense attention, requires a high degree of communication proficiency.

Police Talk offers concise, up-to-date instruction for recruits and officers facing these challenges. Each chapter contains a summary and multiple-choice questions (with answers at the back of the book) to ensure comprehension and reinforce learning. Scenarios and discussion questions bring the realities of modern police work right into the classroom. Every officer, from the newest recruit to the most experienced veteran, can benefit from the information—always practical and often lifesaving—provided in this workbook.

Jean Reynolds is a professional writer and a communications specialist. She has a Ph.D. from the University of South Florida. Her teaching experience includes communication training for the Department of Corrections in Florida. Major Mary Mariani of the Winter Haven Police Department is one of only 35 instructors in domestic violence who have been recognized by the National Association of Women in Policing. A trainer with both a national and an international reputation, she recently traveled to the Republic of Moldova as an expert on women's issues. She holds a Ph.D. from

LaSalle University. Both Mary Mariani and Jean Reynolds are adjuncts in the Criminal Justice Academy at Polk Community College in Winter Haven, Florida.

Acknowledgments

Many people helped to make this book possible, including Kim Davies, Debbie Goodman, and Corey Good at Prentice Hall, and Janet Kiefer at Carlisle Publishers Services. Mary also thanks Sandy Hall, whose friendship and encouragement helped make this book possible; Mella Thornhill, her mom, who has always supported her in all of her endeavors; and her brothers and their families, especially Doug, whose advice and guidance she values and depends upon. Jean thanks Charlie Reynolds, as always, for his encouragement and support. Most of all, we want to thank each other for years of friendship and a productive collaboration.

CHAPTER ONE

INTRODUCTION TO COMMUNICATION

The Importance of Communication

Criminal justice professionals are finding that communication skills are more important than ever before. As the field becomes more complex and sophisticated, officers must rely more on skills and less on strength and force. The old stereotype of the officer as a lone crusader for justice is rapidly disappearing. Today's agencies are seeking recruits who are service oriented rather than adventure oriented.

Law enforcement requires both accountability and teamwork; they, in turn, depend upon communication skills. Tricks and gimmicks will not do the job. You, the officer, must be prepared to develop your abilities through study and practice. Your communication training will draw upon all your experiences with other people, both on and off the job, and it will be an ongoing, lifelong project.

1. Effective communication conveys the message that you are a professional.

By learning to speak and write well, you can earn a reputation as a competent officer. The ability to organize information and express yourself clearly, accurately, and grammatically, especially in written reports, can help you climb the career ladder. The same skills will help you convey a positive message about yourself in oral communication. Whatever the situation, your words can tell others that you are competent, credible, and in control. Over time, your communication skills create an image that you will take with you throughout your career.

1

If professional communication feels alien and unnatural to you, choose a respected officer to emulate. In tense situations, ask what your model would do, and act accordingly. Imitation can help you overcome the anxiety that often accompanies a change in behavior.

2. Communication skills are your first line of defense in potentially dangerous situations.

Effective communication can help you prevent violence. Used effectively, spoken words create a professional image that establishes your authority and encourages cooperation. In a crisis, a single officer may be working alone to control a group of citizens. Cooperation is essential, and your ability to command respect is a key element. Your problem-solving skills can defuse tense situations, protecting both you and those present from violence.

Citizens who respect you and your agency are more cooperative in criminal investigations and less likely to resort to violence against the police. When a community loses respect for police officers, it inevitably loses respect for the law as well.

Communication is especially important when you may have to deal with the use of force. First, officers who communicate well are less likely to have to resort to force. If force does become necessary, your own words may protect you in a subsequent investigation. In one recent case, a suspect complained that he had been injured when an officer handcuffed him. Investigators discovered that the officer had forcibly pulled the suspect's hands without first telling him to put his hands behind his back. A simple oral command might have prevented the injury—and saved the officer from disciplinary action.

In another case, an officer made racist slurs against a suspect at a crime scene. Then other problems arose that led to a disciplinary hearing later on. Bystanders testified against the officer, arguing that he was too prejudiced to treat the suspect fairly. Once again, the result was disciplinary action.

Words can be lifesaving. For your own safety, you should always attempt to communicate with suspects who seem to be unconscious. More than one officer has been shot by a "dead" suspect. Before you approach, give this command: "I'm a police officer. Do not move." In any risky situation, consider whether an appropriate oral message might help protect you from danger.

3. Communication skills are essential to career advancement.

Leadership is not just a matter of power. It also includes the ability to solve problems and inspire confidence. As your career advances, you may find yourself talking and writing to community leaders from many professional areas—politics, religion, education, social welfare, the media, and the judiciary. The time you invest in communication training now can pay tremendous dividends throughout your career.

Some officers mistakenly think that they can forget about professionalism in a low-income neighborhood. The truth is that the way you treat less prominent members of the community can help or harm your career. If you lose your reputation for fairness and professionalism, you may find it difficult—even impossible—to gain back the community's respect.

Questions for Discussion

1. Some officers are concerned that politeness will weaken their authority. Do you agree or disagree? Why?

2. Explain how an officer can use words to defuse a potentially dangerous situation.

Ten Guidelines for Effective Communication

1. Develop an appreciation for the power of language.

Criminal justice is always challenging and often dangerous. Frequently you will have only a few seconds to take control of the situation. The right combination of courtesy and caution puts you in charge. For example, addressing citizens as "Sir" or "Ma'am"—even if they are suspects—may prevent aggressive behavior. Your professionalism may prompt citizens to share information that can be helpful in a criminal investigation. Good grammar and a moderate tone of voice quickly convey a positive message about you.

2. Avoid language that triggers fear, anger, or inferiority in others.

Jargon and sophisticated words can cause others to feel intimidated and uncooperative. Racist, ethnic, and sexist insults can inflame suspects and bystanders. Lying, bragging, threats, and displays of power can escalate a routine incident, such as a traffic stop, into a life-threatening situation. Crude and blasphemous language is always inappropriate for officers. First, professionalism is the key to maintaining order. Furthermore, you don't want to place yourself on the same level as the offender you're confronting—or be accused of causing a minor incident to escalate into violence. Self-control and professionalism should always guide your behavior.

3. Think of "language" in broad terms.

Body language is important. Eye contact, nodding, and attentive listening create a professional image even when someone else is talking. If you are trying to create trust, put yourself on the same physical level as those to whom you are talking. For example, don't stand while talking to a seated person. Sit or bend if possible. Be aware that sunglasses block eye contact and may create a hostile impression. If you want to put a citizen at ease during an interview, choose a setting where there are no physical objects between you, and place yourself at a slight angle. If, on the other hand, you want to create an impression of authority, face a suspect squarely and move in as close as you safely can—backing away can convey a message of fear.

4. In tense situations, foster cooperation before you resort to force.

No matter where you work, you can expect to intervene between two or more angry persons. Your attitude and behavior may determine how the antagonists behave toward one another—and toward you. Patience and politeness relieve tension, save time, and prevent violence.

5. Learn to use words as a problem-solving tool.

A few well-chosen words can make a suspect reevaluate a situation and decide to cooperate. For example, angry suspects who attempt violence against you may not be thinking clearly enough to consider the consequences. But they may decide to cooperate if you issue an effective warning, such as "Sir! Stop resisting arrest!" Such commands also help convince bystanders that you are trying to avoid the use of force. Their testimony may be important if your actions are investigated later on.

When you are dealing with a suspect who is resisting your authority, words can be useful tools. For example, say "Down on the ground!" before (or while) you force a suspect to submit. If he or she submits, you will have avoided the use of force. If not, witnesses will testify that you tried to avoid violence.

Any time you are dealing with a confused or uncooperative person, it may be helpful to ask, "Do you understand what I'm saying?" Patiently repeating information, or restating it more simply and clearly, can have a calming effect. Many officers also use a technique called "distraction" to relieve tension. Instead of plunging into the issue at hand, ask a few general questions. Arguing spouses, for example, may be willing to tell you the names and ages of their children and other facts about their home and family. Interviews are excellent tools for restoring order. Because thinking and feeling are different neurological functions, a person who is answering factual questions is likely to put emotions aside.

6. Whenever practical, inform citizens of the procedures you are following.

A brief, factual description of the procedure inspires trust and cooperation. Citizens who understand what you are doing and why (even if they disagree) are less likely to lose control than citizens who are mystified by police procedures. The explanation can be a simple one, like "I'm calling for a backup" or "I'm tagging this weapon for the evidence room at the station house." Crime victims, who are often overlooked in the criminal justice system, especially appreciate the sharing of information.

Verbalizing your actions is particularly important when you are restraining suspects. Do not assume that suspects understand, without words, what you want them to do. To minimize resistance and prevent violence, issue simple commands when you are patting down, restraining, or placing a suspect in your vehicle. During a civil disobedience demonstration (at an abortion clinic, for example), you may need to arrest persons who are passively resisting the law. To prevent injuries, instruct demonstrators to go limp as you carry them from the area.

7. Monitor your own thoughts to prevent hasty judgments and overreactions.

Positive self-talk can help you face a problem with a clear head and a professional attitude. As you approach a tense situation, recall incidents from the past that you handled well. If you feel yourself becoming anxious, look for prejudgments and stereotyped attitudes that could limit your ability to think. Then switch to positive self-talk ("I know I'm an effective problem solver").

6

8. *Keep your feelings under control.*

Fear, anger, and grief are natural human reactions, but they can interfere with your professional responsibilities. Two or three slow, deep breaths can sometimes relieve tension and help you maintain your professional calm. Experienced officers recommend tightening your diaphragm—the large muscular area under your rib cage—as an aid to self-control. This technique will help you speak calmly during difficult moments and perform your duties effectively.

9. *Put yourself in the other person's place.*

Big words and long, complicated sentences may be frightening to a person who is nervous about talking to an officer. Even citizens with above-average intelligence may experience confusion and memory loss at a crime scene. Use short sentences and clear, simple language as much as possible. This advice is particularly important when you are talking to children, hearing-impaired people, the elderly and infirm, and non-native English speakers.

Be sensitive to a citizen's need for privacy and respect, especially when you are interviewing a victim. Too many officers adopt an aggressive, hostile tone when they are trying to sort out the facts about a crime. Be courteous, respectful, and professional. Make the person as comfortable as possible, away from eavesdroppers and curious onlookers. Take your time. A frightened, hurting person feels worse when rushed. Don't be afraid of silence; pauses allow victims to organize their thoughts and recall vital information.

10. *Use language to build a positive image for yourself and your agency.*

Although a police call may seem routine to you, it is usually a very serious matter to the person who contacted your agency. Citizens may become frustrated and angry when you explain that their problem is not a police matter. What you can do is offer an alternative—a referral to a community agency, an offer to keep an eye on their

7

house that evening, or a follow-up phone call. Inform yourself about community services, and be prepared to provide names and telephone numbers when necessary.

Questions for Discussion

1. Think of a situation in which a person in authority used words effectively to solve a problem. What can you learn from that person's example?

2. Think of a situation in which a person in authority used words that made a problem worse. What can you learn from that person's example?

Summary

1. Effective communication benefits officers by:

   —helping to create a professional image,

   —serving as the first line of defense in a crisis, and

   —aiding officers as they advance in their careers.

2. When danger is present, verbal skills establish authority, win cooperation, and defuse tense situations.

3. Officers should avoid language that triggers fear, anxiety, or inferiority in others.

4. Officers can inspire trust and respect by:

   —using effective body language,

   —courteously explaining procedures when appropriate, and

   —putting themselves into the other person's place.

Multiple Choice Questions

1. Which attitude is most appropriate for an officer?

a) Police procedures are the agency's concern, not the public's.

b) Actions speak louder than words.

c) Effective communication combines courtesy and caution.

d) It's important to use official-sounding words and expressions whenever possible.

2. Which principle does *not* apply when an officer is dealing with a suspect?

a) Inappropriate language may escalate the situation into violence.

b) The officer's job is to apprehend the suspect, not talk.

c) Bystanders form either a positive or negative impression of the officer and agency.

d) Oral commands and explanations may protect the officer, suspect, and public.

3. The best reason for using simple, clear language is that

a) clarity builds understanding.

b) there's always a danger of mispronouncing big words.

c) it's wrong to use a word if you can't spell or define it.

d) complicated language is time consuming to use.

4. Courtesy and professionalism

a) build public confidence in you and your agency.

b) may cause problems when you're dealing with a suspect.

c) may give you an advantage if you're in a situation that is investigated later on.

d) a and c.

5. Taking time to talk with a citizen who has a problem

   a) wastes taxpayers' money.

   b) builds confidence in your agency.

   c) reduces crime rates.

   d) can damage an agency's reputation for toughness on crime.

CHAPTER TWO

COMMUNICATING AUTHORITY

The Use of Authority

Authority and control are often associated with criminal justice. Many drivers ease up on the gas pedal when they spot a patrol car; bystanders often come to attention when they glimpse an officer's uniform. This association with authority has both advantages and disadvantages.

Authority has a positive effect when it prompts cooperation and conformity. Because you are expected to take charge, you may quickly take control at a disturbance or crime scene. Your uniform is a powerful reminder of our country's commitment to law and order. The negative effect occurs when people project their resentment of authority onto an officer, so that a routine incident can escalate into a life-threatening confrontation.

Your own safety, and the welfare of others, requires you to evaluate and refine your image as an authority figure. This principle is especially important when you're dealing with offenders, who tend to harbor long-standing resentment against authority.

Negative Uses of Authority

Projections are images that a person unconsciously places on another person. Projections cause people to lose touch with the reality of a situation. They respond to a mental picture rather than the actual person. For example, suppose you resemble a suspect's abusive father. During the arrest, the suspect may become violent toward you

11

because she has unconsciously confused you with her father. Offenders often project negative qualities onto authority figures.

Stereotyping occurs when people make generalizations that ignore individual differences. Your name, ethnic group, social class, age, size, or sex may trigger negative reactions. Some citizens are fearful of large men and try to protect themselves through aggressive behavior. Others dislike women and try to intimidate them through sexual threats and obscene language. Ethnic stereotypes are a particular problem because our society is still struggling to integrate blacks, whites, and other groups. Any of these situations can add serious complications to routine police and corrections work.

Overreaction occurs when a person has an exaggerated response to a situation. For example, an officer may wrongly expect violence in a situation where there is little actual danger. Unnecessary use of force is often triggered by such overreactions. If you have just completed a call involving a dangerous suspect, you may overreact to the next citizen you meet, especially if you notice a similarity in sex, size, or ethnic group. In the same way, citizens may still be harboring anger from their last encounter with an officer. Such situations may quickly become dangerous.

Repetitive behavior patterns occur when people rely on a favorite manipulative behavior to obtain what they want—threats, insults, irrational behavior, and so on. (See Chapter 3.) Dealing with these ingrained patterns (often learned in childhood) can be highly stressful for an officer. In some families, for example, an exaggerated sense of honor requires men to react aggressively when they have been embarrassed in front of others, even at the risk of injury or death. As a result, an officer may be injured or even killed over a small issue. Some people—especially women—have been trained since childhood not to think for themselves; others feel obligated to disobey even the most reasonable requests from an authority figure. Learning how to deal with these patterns can be lifesaving for an officer.

Overidentification occurs when a person loses touch with his or her individuality to identify with someone more impressive. For example, gang members often emulate a street hero, imitating his behavior without thinking about the consequences. Overidentification can also happen to officers, who may unconsciously copy a role model from a TV show or movie. The obvious problem is that media entertainment is vastly different from the complexities of real police work. Unconscious role-playing can lead to serious errors in judgment.

Questions for Discussion

1. List as many "repetitive behavior patterns" as you can think of. What repeated emotions are involved?

2. What common attitudes towards authority figures can create problems for officers?

Communicating Authority

Your speech and bearing can help you handle many negative situations safely. As you saw in Chapter 1, experienced officers know the importance of creating the right image, especially during the first few minutes of a call. The following six suggestions will help you deal with challenges to your authority:

1. Avoid power contests, which can escalate an ordinary call into a life-threatening confrontation.

When possible, ignore baiting from suspects and witnesses. Do not provoke them to feel that they must redeem their honor by attacking you. Do not attempt to "reform" someone whose attitude or behavior offends you, and avoid using intimidation to control a dangerous person. Call for backup assistance instead. Your job is to maintain order, protect others, safeguard property, and follow the procedures you have been given. Do not assume the role of a lone crusader for justice. Remember that the only person whose behavior you can control is your own. When dealing with other people, you are limited to offering choices and enforcing consequences.

2. Avoid overidentifying with your own authority.

Do not fantasize excessively about media police heroes. Keep in touch with your individuality and humanity by having interests and associations outside criminal justice. On the job, be wary of absorbing inappropriate attitudes toward others. Off-the-cuff "station house" talk is a great stress reducer, but it also has risks. Maintain your professionalism, and choose your role models carefully.

3. Do not deliberately trigger hostile feelings in citizens or inmates.

Avoid blatant shows of power, such as swaggering, taunts, and insults. Don't go out of your way to humiliate others. Your threatening words may provoke others to flaunt their own power or defend their honor, with deadly results.

4. Remember that professionalism is your first line of defense.

Both citizens and offenders are less likely to be influenced by projections when they respect your authority. Follow the procedures you have been taught, keep your emotions under control, and maintain your objectivity. Politeness mingled with firmness can help you avoid being drawn into arguments and power contests.

5. Remember that the only behavior you can control is your own.

Vowing to teach someone a lesson, reform another person, or instill a principle important to you is usually a losing battle. You can't remake a person's character or change anyone's belief system. Staking your self-esteem on a desired change in another person puts you in a weak position. It is almost impossible to force another person to do what you want. Physical threats are the exception, but even they will not change another person's thinking, attitude, or beliefs.

6. *Know your agency's policies, follow and enforce them, and be prepared to follow up with the appropriate consequences.*

Be prepared for the reality that other people—especially offenders—may not do what you want them to do. Don't lose your dignity over a showdown or power contest.

Questions for Discussion

1. How might an angry citizen "bait" an officer? Why? What principles should the officer keep in mind to maintain control of the situation?

2. What are the risks when an officer imagines himself or herself as a hero?

Summary

1. Citizens may respond to police authority in both positive and negative ways.

2. Manipulative patterns such as projection, stereotyping, overreaction, repetitive behaviors, and overidentification put both officers and citizens at risk.

3. Officers can use their authority to protect both themselves and the public.

Multiple-Choice Questions

1. An officer has a reputation for never admitting he's wrong. Which behavior pattern is he using?

   a) stereotyping

   b) power contest

   c) projection

   d) repetitive behavior pattern

2. What attitude toward authority is most appropriate for an officer?

   a) I'm in charge and can do whatever I want.

   b) I strive to make a positive impression with my skills and knowledge.

   c) A courteous officer is a weak officer.

   d) I always shout a few orders right away to establish my authority.

3. An officer always stops minority drivers in high-income neighborhoods. Which behavior pattern is she using?

   a) stereotyping

   b) power contest

   c) projection

   d) repetitive behavior pattern

4. You are working with an officer who has just transferred from another agency where she assisted with sex-abuse investigations. You notice that she is uneasy and suspicious of men. Which behavior pattern is she using?

   a) stereotyping

   b) power contest

   c) projection

   d) repetitive behavior pattern

5. An officer stops a vehicle for running a stop sign. The driver is a black male about 18 years old. The officer immediately places his hand on his service weapon. What behavior is this officer exhibiting?

a) overidentification

b) projection

c) overreaction

d) power contest

CHAPTER THREE

DEALING WITH MANIPULATION

Introduction to Manipulation

Manipulation is the attempt to get one's needs met through inappropriate means. Manipulative strategies include the use of guilt, helplessness, flattery, and anger. This chapter will teach you how to recognize manipulation and counter it through assertive responses.

Everyone wants to feel important and receive attention from others. Mature people use healthy means to get these needs met. People with dysfunctional personalities, on the other hand, often rely on manipulation to get what they want. No matter how serious the consequences are, many people can't resist the short-lived thrill of a power contest with authority.

Deeply ingrained manipulative habits account for much of the apparently bewildering behavior seen in offenders. Some offenders deliberately break laws in order to get attention. The temporary excitement of a confrontation with an officer helps break up the monotonous emptiness of their lives, and they may experience a short-lived sense of power during a conflict with an officer.

Dealing Effectively with Manipulation

Assertiveness is the key to dealing effectively with manipulation. Assertiveness is defined as honest, goal-directed communication. An assertive officer calmly and quietly maintains control of a situation despite attempts at manipulation from other people. The officer refuses to be sidetracked by arguments, name-calling, baiting, helplessness, flattery, or other ploys.

While you are learning new assertive skills, keep this sentence in mind: Stay focused on your goal! These five words keep you in touch with the basic principle of assertiveness: honest, goal-directed communication. Whether you are searching a vehicle, examining a driver's license, or settling a domestic dispute, do not allow yourself to be distracted by verbal sidetracking. Your ability to focus will help you maintain order, perform an efficient investigation, and protect yourself and others.

What's Different about Assertiveness?

It's important to distinguish among *assertiveness, aggression,* and *submission.* The goal of *aggression* is control through power. Aggressive communication attempts to master a situation through force—shouting, anger, threats, shame, or intimidation. Aggressive communication is always mistaken in its goals for two reasons. First, no one can ever have absolute power over another person. Many people have died rather than perform an act against their will. As many officers have painfully learned, power showdowns can have embarrassing outcomes. Second, aggression adds nothing to an officer's authority, which derives from the legal system of the United States.

On the other hand, some officers are so repelled by aggression that they resort to *submission*—apologies, excuses, exaggerated politeness—to solve problems. Officers afraid to take charge are compromising their authority and putting people's lives in danger. For your safety and everyone else's, it is important to understand and practice *assertiveness*—verbal skills that put you in charge without provoking aggressive responses from others.

Questions for Discussion

1. Recall a time when you saw someone use aggression to solve a problem. How could the problem have been handled more assertively?

2. Recall a time when you saw someone use submission to solve a problem. How could the problem have been handled more assertively?

Three Useful Assertiveness Skills

1. "I" messages.

To head off arguments, state *objective facts*—not opinions—from your own point of view. Avoid labels and other inflammatory language. Compare these two responses:

   a) OFFICER: Sir, you were driving recklessly. [inflammatory]

   b) OFFICER: Sir, I saw your vehicle cross the double line five times in the past two minutes. [effective "I" message]

Not all "I" messages are assertive. It would still be inflammatory if the officer had said, "I saw you driving recklessly." Effective "I" messages are objective statements of the reality observed or experienced by the speaker.

2. "Broken record."

This skill helps you maintain control by stating a position and repeating it as many times as needed. ("I" messages can be helpful here as well.) The repeated phrases and sentences sound like a "broken record," giving this useful skill its name.

   CITIZEN: I was going only fifty back there.

OFFICER: Sir, I clocked you at sixty-five.

CITIZEN: It's not fair to give me a ticket because my speedometer was broken.

OFFICER: I'm not going to argue. I clocked you at sixty-five. [broken record]

CITIZEN: Don't you cops have better things to do with your time than harassing taxpayers like me?

OFFICER: Sir, I clocked you at sixty-five, and I'm writing a ticket. [broken record]

In this situation, the officer maintained order and professionalism by refusing to be drawn into an argument. Conflict is an unavoidable component of criminal justice—but it can often be kept under control through effective communication skills.

Effective broken record responses include the following:

"The radar shows . . . ."

"The car didn't stop at the intersection."

"I'm not going to argue."

"That's for the court to decide."

3. Negative assertion.

In this skill, you partially agree with a negative statement made by another person. Although negative assertion is inappropriate in many types of confrontations, it is useful when you want to soften a stressful situation. For example, if someone threatens suicide because of an unfaithful lover, the officer can make a negative assertion: "She shouldn't have treated you that way." A broken record message can follow: "But that's no reason to kill yourself."

Negative assertion can sometimes stop an argument before it begins.

CITIZEN: I didn't know this was a school zone. Why doesn't it have a blinking light?

OFFICER: [negative assertion] That might be a good suggestion to bring before the school board. Here are your license and registration, Ma'am, and here's your ticket. We want to protect the children who go to school here.

Negative assertion is especially useful when you are teaching or supervising. It facilitates communication between you and your subordinates without compromising your role as an authority figure.

OFFICER: Sarge, I'm getting really angry at the prosecutor's office. They threw another one of my cases out. This really makes my conviction record look bad.

SERGEANT: [negative assertion] I can understand why you're frustrated. Conviction rates play a part in your overall performance evaluation. Have you looked at the possible reasons they might have for not prosecuting your cases? Let me look at one of your reports on a case that got thrown out. Maybe we can work together to improve your report writing. I know that you do good investigations. Maybe the problem is how you present those cases on paper.

With practice, the assertiveness techniques you learned in this chapter can help you deal with many on-the-job communications problems.

Questions for Discussion

1. Recall a time when you could have used broken record to interrupt a manipulative situation. What could you have said to break the pattern?

2. Give an example of a time when you might use negative assertion; then give an example of a situation in which you would definitely not use negative assertion.

Summary

1. Assertiveness is an effective alternative to aggressive and submissive communication.

2. Officers need to know how to recognize and deal with "verbal sidetracking" from citizens.

3. "I" messages, "broken record," and "negative assertion" are useful assertive techniques.

Multiple-Choice Questions

1. You tell a driver that she has to move her car, which is parked next to a fire hydrant. She complains that it's too far to walk on such a hot day. You agree that it is indeed very hot today. Your response is an example of

   a) negative assertion.

   b) submission.

   c) aggression.

   d) manipulation.

2. A lounge owner reports a fight between two patrons. The officer at the scene asks one of the men to step into the dining room, adding, "I need to interview you, if you don't mind." The officer is using

   a) aggression.

   b) broken record.

   c) "I" message.

   d) submission.

3. At a traffic stop, the driver repeatedly tries to persuade the officer not to write a ticket. The officer keeps saying, "I'm not going to argue with you." The officer is using

   a) aggression.

b) broken record.

c) "I" message.

d) submission.

4. Which of the following is an example of an assertive response?

a) "I think you're lying."

b) "You must be really stupid if you think you can make me change my mind."

c) "I'm carrying out my agency's procedure."

d) "I'm not going to let you tell me what to do."

5. "If you do not sit down and shut up, I'm going to tape your mouth shut." This statement is an example of

a) assertiveness.

b) aggression.

c) submission.

d) a power contest.

CHAPTER FOUR

THE RESCUE TRIANGLE

Introducing the Rescue Triangle

The "rescue triangle" is a manipulative, unconscious behavior pattern that appears frequently in three-person confrontations. Originally identified by Eric Berne, author of *Games People Play,* the rescue triangle has become an important training tool for professionals in many fields, including counseling and law enforcement. The rescue triangle frequently occurs in a domestic dispute because an officer is often the third person involved. But it can develop any time an officer intervenes between two disputants—for example, in confrontations between neighbors, friends, relatives, business partners, and other situations.

Rescue triangle theory says that people tend to play three manipulative roles: persecutor, victim, and rescuer. As the tension builds during a conflict, the roles may switch rapidly until they finally erupt into an explosion. Here's an example of how the three roles might work in a typical family:

MOTHER: Billy, this is a disgraceful report card. [persecuting Billy]

BILLY: I don't know what's wrong, Mom. I can't seem to do better. [victim]

DAD: Linda, shut up and get off the kid's back. At least he's not on drugs. [rescuing Billy; persecuting Mom]

BILLY: Dad, leave Mom alone. At least she cares about me. [rescuing Mom; persecuting Dad]

DAD: Don't you dare speak to me like that! I'll teach you some respect. [persecuting Billy]

It's not difficult to see how this family might go out of control. Dad may attack Billy, who may become violent himself. If Mom tries to stop Dad, she too may be drawn into violence.

When an officer steps into a domestic conflict, he or she may be unconsciously drawn into the pattern as a persecutor, rescuer, or victim, as in this example:

MR. BROWN: Shut up, you bitch, or I'll hit you again.

OFFICER: Mrs. Brown, your husband is a dangerous man. You need to get away from this house, now. [rescuing Mrs. Brown; persecuting Mr. Brown]

MRS. BROWN: You have no right to criticize my husband! You're not a tenth the man that he is. [rescuing Mr. Brown; persecuting the officer]

Once again, violence may follow—and this time the helpful officer may be the victim. Of course there is nothing wrong with genuinely rescuing someone who has truly been victimized—a person who has been robbed, assaulted, or raped. Similarly there is nothing wrong with prosecuting a criminal. The decisive factor in the rescue triangle is manipulation.

Even when family members experience conflicts outside the home, they may fall into the same inflammatory behaviors. The rescue triangle occurs in many community settings, with the same potential for violence. When an officer appears on the scene as the third party, the pattern may erupt with life-threatening force. By educating yourself about the rescue triangle, you can help protect yourself and others when handling many types of conflicts.

1. Explain the difference between a victim of a crime and a person manipulatively playing the role of victim in the rescue triangle.

2. Some people use helplessness as a way to avoid responsibility. List three situations in which a citizen might use this manipulative ploy.

Avoiding the Rescue Triangle

To avoid becoming part of the triangle yourself, separate arguing couples and pairs if possible. Calling for a backup, or working with a partner, can be helpful because there are four participants now instead of just three.

Practice identifying rescue triangle behaviors in yourself and in others. Chastising and condemning are "persecutor" actions; oversympathizing is a "rescuer" trait. All three can trigger violence.

The safest course is to deal factually, not emotionally, with tense situations:

OFFICER: Mr. Brown, it's not wise for you to stay here with your wife now. Where else can you spend the night? [realistic response]

OFFICER: Mrs. Brown, that cut needs medical attention. I'm calling for an ambulance. Then we need to select a safe place for you to spend the night. [realistic response]

Other Forms of the Rescue Triangle

Manipulative role-playing often slips into working relationships between officers. Extreme helplessness is one example of "victim" behavior that can create problems. A trainee may seek extra attention from a field training officer (FTO) because of exaggerated nervousness, low self-esteem, or insufficient experience. At first the FTO enjoys the helping role, feeling virtuous and important. But eventually the good feelings weaken, the FTO feels overburdened and used, and the rescuer evolves into a persecutor. Or a trainee who has been playing a victim role resents the FTO's stream of well-meaning advice and suggestions. Again a shift to the role of persecutor may follow.

How to Apply the Rescue Triangle

1. Do not overextend yourself in helping relationships.

Make sure the person you're helping is investing time and energy equal to yours. Don't repeatedly perform an unpleasant or difficult task because someone else in your agency doesn't want to do it. Disproportionate kindness often develops into anger and persecutor role-playing.

2. Use particular caution in any confrontation with two angry people, both inside and outside your agency.

Think about the risks and consequences before you become involved in someone else's problem—unless it's part of your official responsibilities.

3. Stick closely to official procedures.

Many offenders routinely bait officers with insulting language and gestures. Often the officer becomes angry and takes on the persecutor role; then the offender becomes a victim, complaining loudly about mistreatment. Clever offenders can use this scenario to bring charges against officers and ruin their careers. You can avoid this trap by maintaining professional standards. Do not blame, argue with, or shame suspects or witnesses. Don't allow yourself to be victimized. Focus solely on your goal: to complete your investigation and take whatever action is appropriate.

Questions for Discussion

1. How can an understanding of the rescue triangle be helpful to officers who do not often handle domestic disputes?

2. Explain how an officer's unprofessional behavior might set up a rescue triangle.

Summary

1. The rescue triangle is a manipulative pattern, often involving three people, that can escalate into violence.

2. Officers can safeguard themselves and others by sticking to agency procedures and avoiding blaming, shaming, and over-sympathizing.

3. The rescue triangle can be particularly dangerous in domestic disputes.

Multiple-Choice Questions

1. A single mother asks an officer to come to her home and lecture her 13-year-old son, who has become difficult to control. The officer confronts the boy as asked. The next day, the mother calls the chief to complain that the officer's warnings were excessive and the boy's behavior is worse. In this situation, the officer played the roles of

   a) victim and persecutor.

   b) rescuer and victim.

   c) rescuer and persecutor.

   d) rescuer, victim, and persecutor.

2. The rescue triangle is likely to happen when

   a) a person is victimized by a criminal.

   b) two people make an equal effort to solve a problem.

c) three people are involved in a confrontation.

d) an agency is prosecuting a criminal.

3. An elderly man calls the police because teens in his neighborhood are annoying him. The responding officer tells him there are no grounds for charges against the teens. She suggests setting up an informal meeting with one of the teen leaders to work out the problems. Which role in the rescue triangle is she playing?

a) rescuer

b) victim

c) persecutor

d) none

4. In the rescue triangle,

a) participants usually switch roles.

b) the officer is usually the persecutor.

c) the officer is usually the victim.

d) the officer is usually the rescuer.

5. Officers should avoid being drawn into the rescue triangle because

a) officers are supposed to prosecute lawbreakers, not rescue them.

b) it's wrong to prosecute victims.

c) the dynamics of the rescue triangle can be deadly.

d) "rescuing" is the responsibility of other agencies.

CHAPTER FIVE

LISTENING AND INTERVIEWING SKILLS

The Importance of Listening

Many officers underestimate the importance of listening. In a tense situation, it may seem passive to remain silent while giving full attention to what another person is saying. The impulse to speak out forcefully, rather than listening in silence, is hard to resist.

However, good listening skills are essential to good law enforcement. An officer who listens well soon develops a reputation for accuracy and trustworthiness. Information acquired through listening can be useful in resolving citizen disputes and pursuing complex investigations. Listening is particularly important during interviews. Good listening skills facilitate the whole process of gathering and verifying information.

Developing these skills requires self-discipline and concentration, and progress may be slow at first. With time, the energy you invest will pay handsome dividends. Effective listening will help you enhance your professional image, write better reports, solve problems more efficiently, communicate more effectively, and maintain better control as you perform your duties.

Questions for Discussion

1. Describe a person you know whom you consider a good listener. List the qualities that make you feel comfortable and confident talking to him or her.

2. Recall a time when you tried to communicate something important to a person who did not take you seriously. How did you feel? What were the consequences?

Essential Interviewing Skills

1. Preparation.

Before you begin an interview, arrange an appropriate setting. Both you and the person you're talking to should be seated comfortably so that you're both at eye level. In an investigation, privacy is essential; so is trust. If you are trying to establish rapport, avoid having physical barriers between you, such as a vase of flowers, briefcase, or desk. Such objects inhibit communication.

Remember that you are being judged. Your actions should demonstrate that you're a trustworthy professional. Experienced officers often begin an interview with courteous, casual conversation about a subject of mutual interest—sports, unusual weather, or family life. In a person's home, you can admire some feature of the architecture, setting, or furnishings. Avoid controversial subjects such as politics, religion, or social problems.

In dealing with a victim, allow some time for feelings to be ventilated. You don't have to offer solutions to the problems at hand. Nod encouragingly, make eye contact, and express your concern. Then, at an appropriate time, say, "I'd like to get the facts about what happened" and begin your interview.

2. Concentration.

If you're not paying attention, you may miss something important— a fact, a feeling, or other vital information. Factual errors caused by inattention can be especially embarrassing in court. Even if you're simply discussing an everyday problem with a citizen, poor listening skills may damage your image.

Most people have never fully developed their listening potential. Fortunately, concentration increases with practice, and opportunities to improve occur constantly. The next time you attend a movie, watch a TV news show, or eavesdrop on a conversation, practice tuning in completely to what is said. Test yourself by trying to repeat what you heard. This simple self-improvement program can (and should) be a lifetime project—one that will reward your efforts again and again.

3. Focusing.

Listening is difficult when someone rambles, overwhelms you with irrelevant information, or talks incoherently. When you interview an anxious citizen at a crime scene, you may have trouble sorting out the jumble of events and facts you are hearing. You can improve your listening comprehension by making your own connections between the citizen's information and your observations at the scene. Appropriate questions (but not too many) can be helpful as well.

You may find it helpful to list five headings, with space after each, on your notepad when you begin your investigation: victims, witnesses, suspects, evidence, and disposition. By entering facts under the appropriate headings, you will experience less confusion when you are recording information.

4. Neutrality.

Don't let preconceptions weaken your listening skills. Train yourself to set aside your opinions when you are listening. This advice is particularly important when the speaker is different from you in some significant way. Don't allow yourself to be influenced by ethnic, economic, religious, sexual, or educational barriers. A person who is mentally ill, unemployed, or disabled may provide valuable information. Biases about a person's age, lifestyle, or previous history can prevent you from learning important facts.

Avoid exposing your own attitude toward what you're hearing. Don't influence a citizen's statement by nodding, asking leading questions, or excitedly taking notes about the details you find important. Don't immediately challenge a statement that seems deceptive. A defensive, argumentative witness is unlikely to help your investigation. When the citizen has completed his or her statement, you can choose an appropriate way to deal with the deception.

5. Accuracy.

Many officers mentally divide interviews into two parts: storytelling and verification. They find it helpful to allow witnesses to tell their stories freely, with a minimum of interruptions for questions and notetaking. In the second phase of the interview, they verify the facts, ask questions about gaps in the story, and record basic information: names, addresses, and so on. Premature or excessive notetaking can be an obstacle to communication. Try to record most of your notes near the end of the interview.

6. Decoding mixed messages.

Sometimes a speaker will communicate one message through words and a contradictory one through body language. For example, a suspect may assure you that she's not angry and has no desire to hurt anyone. But her loud voice, aggressive posture, and clenched fists may convey a different message. Similarly a battered woman may refuse to press charges against her husband, insisting that the dispute was a minor one. But you may perceive fear in her anxious eyes, nervous hands, and quavering voice. When in doubt, trust body language rather than verbal messages.

7. Closing the interview.

Don't be too abrupt. Ask if there's any other information to be shared—you may learn valuable information that way—and thank the person for cooperating. Many officers close an interview on a professional note by offering a business card in case further communication is necessary.

Reflective Listening

Reflective listening (also called *active listening*) is one of the most useful skills an officer can possess. As you listen, you reflect (repeat) what you have heard; then you pause while the speaker confirms or corrects your statement:

> OFFICER: So you saw a young white male wearing a white t-shirt and jeans carrying a small brown paper sack. [reflective listening].
>
> WITNESS: That's right, Officer. [confirmation]

It's easy to see the importance of reflective listening during a criminal investigation. By verifying the information you have heard, you can ensure the accuracy of your report.

Reflective listening has other uses too. It can ease negative emotions, open communication channels, and clarify issues during a disagreement. This versatility makes reflective listening highly useful in FTO programs, teaching, supervision, and leadership.

Experienced officers say that this skill has four important benefits. First, it demonstrates that you are paying attention. Second, it helps speakers clarify their thoughts and feelings. Third, it helps nervous witnesses remember more details and expand their statements. Most important, it relieves you of the burden of offering a solution to every problem you are hearing. Reflective listening is simply that—reflection. You need not (and should not) feel obligated to solve all the problems presented to you.

Do not be fooled by its simplicity. Reflective listening is a powerful tension reducer. Today's stressful world often causes people to experience loneliness, depersonalization, anxiety, and fear. Reflective listening restores their dignity, diminishing their need to act out and lose control. By offering a few moments of respectful attention, you may be able to help others let go of their negative feelings. From there you can often facilitate a peaceful solution to the problem at hand.

Examples.

Summarizing information:

> CITIZEN: The beatings started about two months ago. At first we were very happy. Then he started meeting his friends to drink on weekends. He always gets violent then. I begged him to stop drinking because we always get along fine then. He promised to stop, but he didn't. And now this happened. I can't put up with him anymore.
>
> OFFICER: So drinking is the root of the problem. [summarizing]
>
> CITIZEN: That's right. [verifying]

Clarifying feelings:

> OFFICER: I know I shouldn't have lost my temper the way I did. The driver must think I'm a raving idiot. I didn't tell him I had just worked a traffic crash involving a speeding car that injured a two-year-old. I just flew off when he told me I should be out arresting real criminals, not mere speeders.
>
> SERGEANT: It sounds like you are embarrassed about what happened. I think you wish you had explained the situation to him.

Suggestions for reflective listening.

1. When you are verifying information, stick closely to the speaker's exact words. When you are summarizing or clarifying, however, paraphrase (repeat, but in your own words) what you have heard.

2.   When dealing with negative emotions, encourage the speaker to be as specific as possible. The word *upset* is too general to be useful. As you clarify what you are hearing, offer the speaker words that are more specific, such as *angry, afraid, guilty, ashamed,* or *frustrated.*

3.   Use appropriate body language as you listen. Give the speaker your full attention. Don't fidget, and don't let another task distract you. Lean forward slightly, make eye contact, nod, and uncross your arms. If you're taking notes, move your eyes from the notepad to the speaker whenever possible.

In spite of their simplicity, listening skills are mastered by a relatively small number of people. The ability to listen well immediately sets you apart from others. You create an atmosphere of trust, concern, and professionalism. In addition, listening skills give you access to a wealth of information that can solve a crime, warn you of possible injury, and even save your life. Be assured that the time and effort needed to develop these skills are well worth the investment.

Questions for Discussion

1. Which qualities do you already have that make you a good listener? What skills, strategies, and qualities do you think you need to develop? How do you plan to improve your ability to listen?

2. Describe a situation in which you felt that you were receiving a mixed message. What conflicting messages do you think were being communicated? Why do you think the person was sending a mixed message?

Summary

1. Reflective listening (also called *active listening*) helps to verify and clarify information.

2. Effective listening techniques build trust, defuse tense situations, and enhance an officer's professional image.

3. Interviewing skills can ease victims' suffering and expedite investigations.

Multiple-Choice Questions

1. Detailed notetaking may

   a) compromise your ability to observe.

   b) build trust.

   c) sharpen your writing skills.

   d) shorten interviews.

2. Reflective listening may

   a) increase the accuracy of a report.

   b) build trust.

   c) help victims relax and remember.

   d) all of these.

3. Mixed messages

   a) pack useful information into small units.

   b) make your job easier.

   c) involve oral and body language.

   d) all of these.

4. When you're conducting an interview

   a) efficiency should be your primary goal.

   b) you should take time to prepare the setting.

   c) you should maintain control by doing most of the talking.

   d) you should take abundant notes.

5. Trainers who use reflective listening may
   a) weaken their authority.
   b) gain useful information.
   c) be sidetracked from valuable training opportunities.
   d) all of these.

CHAPTER SIX

SENSITIVITY

The Importance of Sensitivity

Much of your success in law enforcement will be determined by your sensitivity to others, many of whom may be different from you in some way—race, social standing, ethnic group, religion, age, language, or sexual orientation. Many of these people have special needs, including the elderly, people with disabilities, and AIDS patients. The Americans with Disabilities Act has broadened the rights enjoyed by these persons. Crime victims are another group receiving more attention and legal protection from the criminal justice system. In addition, recent demographic changes in the United States are causing minority groups to grow in number—increasing the likelihood that you will encounter individuals different from yourself and your family. Even the ethnic makeup of police departments is changing dramatically in many parts of this country.

As an officer, you are both legally and morally required to respond sensitively to all the citizens you are serving. Make a point of learning and applying the principles and skills described in this chapter. In spite of their simplicity, they are vital to your success in dealing with others.

Questions for Discussion

1. Describe the neighborhood where you grew up. Did it encourage or discourage you from being comfortable with diversity? Why?

2. Recall a time when you felt you were treated with insensitivity because of your youth, lack of experience, or some other factor. How did that experience feel?

Body Language

Even before you've uttered a word, your actions can reveal a great deal about your attitude toward others, especially persons with disabilities.

Effective eye contact can go a long way to building trust. Avoid staring, but do look directly at people when you're talking to them. Keep yourself on eye level as much as possible. When talking to a bedridden person, pull up a chair and sit, not stand, during the conversation. Sit, bend, or squat when talking to a person who uses a wheelchair. Bend your knees to lower yourself to eye level when talking to a child.

Touch can have both negative and positive effects. Avoid any touch or gesture that might suggest sexual aggression or unnecessary force. An action that seems innocent to you may be misunderstood by an observer, leading to disciplinary action.

For your own protection, when using physical restraint, use words to describe what you're doing. Ask for the subject's cooperation even if you don't expect to get it. You decrease your chances of being cited for unnecessary force.

At other times touch can be used positively. Shake hands in normal fashion when you meet an ill or disabled person. Some AIDS patients and minority persons especially dislike being made to feel that they are physically repellent to others. (Remember that AIDS cannot be contracted through touch.)

When you are dealing with disabilities, some special rules apply. Do not adjust or move a wheelchair without asking first. Seek permission before you take a blind or ill person's arm to assist with movement. You can ask, "Would you like me to take your arm and help you?" The recipient will appreciate your thoughtfulness and often can give you instructions about the best way to help. Blind persons, for example, may like being gently steered by the elbow. A person who walks haltingly may wish to lean slightly on your arm.

Other tips: Do not pet or play with a blind person's guide dog—or any service animal. When visiting a bedridden person, don't jar or sit on the bed. When you are around children, ask the parent or guardian (or the child) for permission before picking them up or playing vigorously with them.

Talking

Language is part of the basic machinery of our daily lives. Because of their power, words must be used thoughtfully and sensitively.

1. Avoid labeling.

People with special needs prefer language that grants them dignity and individuality. Avoid phrases that lump people together, such as *the deaf, the blind, the mentally ill.* It's preferable to say "deaf persons" or "persons with a history of mental illness." Many people with illnesses dislike being called victims. It's preferable to use such phrases as *an AIDS patient* or *a person who has epilepsy* instead.

2. Avoid demeaning language.

Do not use disparaging words such as *crazy, deformed, crippled, handicapped, retarded, spastic, afflicted,* or *epileptic.* The word *seizure* is preferable to *fit. Low income* is preferable to *lower class.*

Be sensitive to the feelings of minority groups. No matter what language you heard in your neighborhood as a child, do not use slang to refer to ethnic or religious groups, or persons whose sexual orientation is different from yours. Modern law enforcement requires a sophisticated and professional image. Derogatory language can be a serious impediment to effective communication, promotions, and professional growth.

3. Respect the basic humanity of others.

Persons with special needs have two major complaints about communication. First, others tend to raise their voices unnecessarily. A person who is blind, elderly, or sitting in a wheelchair can usually hear normally. Second, persons with special needs tend to feel ignored and left out of ordinary conversations. They are usually capable of dealing with the ordinary business of living, so talk directly to them whenever possible. Do not address yourself to interpreters, aides, assistants, and family members rather than the person involved.

Keep conversations as normal as possible. It's all right to use the words *walk* and *run* when you speak to wheelchair users. Feel free to say "look" and "see" with a blind or visually impaired person. Smile and face blind persons as you talk. Even without sight, they will notice the difference.

Don't tell persons with special needs that you pity them or admire their courage. Don't say, "It could have been worse" or "God chose you for a special reason." Restrain your curiosity. Don't ask how bodily functions or daily tasks are performed.

Remember that all human beings are fundamentally alike in many ways. People who seem very different are likely to have values similar to yours, and they probably care as much about their family and friends as you do. The flexibility of American life means that a person whose lifestyle is very different from yours could have been your next-door neighbor last year, or may move into your neighborhood before the year is over. Learn to treat others with dignity even if their income, lifestyle, sexual orientation, or ethnic group is different from yours.

43

4. Learn how to deal with special needs.

Hearing-impaired persons often communicate through an interpreter. The procedure to follow is simple but important. Talk directly to the hearing-impaired, using the words *you* and *your* in normal fashion. Don't talk to the interpreter, and don't say "Tell him that. . . ." Some deaf persons prefer to lip-read. Be sure to face the lip-reader directly, and don't cover your mouth with your hand.

Persons with mental retardation appreciate short sentences and simple language. Don't shout—usually they can hear normally.

Listen patiently to persons who stammer or stutter. Do not try to finish their sentences for them. Don't coach them or advise them to relax or slow down. Give them feedback when you don't understand a sentence and need to hear it again. Concentrate on staying relaxed yourself, and you'll be an effective listener.

5. Offer help when appropriate.

For example, a blind person will appreciate knowing who else is present during an interview. Describe the physical setting as well if it is an unfamiliar one.

If you suspect that someone is physically uncomfortable or having mobility problems, offer assistance. Don't go out of your way to pretend that the disability does not exist.

Most important, learn to separate the person from the disability—or any other special circumstances that apply. This principle is the essence of sensitivity, and the key to confident performance of your duties.

Questions for Discussion

1. Which do you think conveys a stronger message to others—verbal language or body language? Why?

2. Imagine that you are visiting a place where you are different from everyone else around you. What apprehensions might you feel? What could others do to make you feel safe and welcome?

Summary

1. All persons have the right to be treated with dignity.

2. Appropriate touch, eye contact, and tactful language can help all citizens feel more comfortable in your presence.

3. A few simple techniques can help you communicate more effectively with persons with impaired hearing or sight.

Multiple Choice Questions

1. Which of the following is *not* a reason for officers to treat others with sensitivity?

   a) The Americans with Disabilities Act

   b) Changing demographics in the United States

   c) Declining respect for police officers

   d) Crime victims are receiving increased attention from criminal justice professionals

2. Which of the following guidelines should you follow during your everyday duties?

   a) People with special needs may be offended if you avoid touching them.

   b) Women appreciate physical contact that makes them feel attractive and desirable.

   c) It's risky to touch a person with AIDS.

   d) Avoid shaking the hand of a person from an ethnic group different from your own.

3. Which of the following guidelines is *not* appropriate?

   a) Keep your eyes level with the eyes of the person to whom you are talking.

   b) Speaking loudly improves communication with disabled persons.

   c) Talk directly to a deaf person, not the interpreter.

   d) Ask before offering help.

4. You are interviewing a blind person in an office at your headquarters. You can build rapport and trust by

   a) playing with the seeing-eye dog.

   b) avoiding words like *look* and *see*.

   c) maintaining eye contact.

   d) describing the office where you're conducting the interview.

5. Treating a homosexual with courtesy

   a) weakens your authority in the eyes of onlookers.

   b) makes onlookers think you're ignorant about homosexuality.

   c) impresses onlookers with your professionalism.

   d) hints that you're a homosexual yourself.

CHAPTER SEVEN

CRIME VICTIMS

Communicating with Crime Victims

In the stress of dealing with crime, the needs and rights of victims are often overlooked. Yet crime victims stand at the very center of the justice system. If a victim refuses to cooperate, a criminal investigation or prosecution may be doomed to failure; unapprehended lawbreakers remain free to prey upon others.

But crime victims often complain of harsh treatment—unnecessary and hostile questioning, insensitivity to their suffering, and a lack of support from the agencies charged with their protection. The price of this insensitivity is high. Some experts estimate that almost half of all violent crimes go unreported because victims mistrust the criminal justice system. Resolve now to treat all victims courteously and compassionately, even if their social status, lifestyle, ethnic group, religion, or sexual orientation is different from yours.

Resolve also to educate yourself about professional standards for dealing with victims. Like everyone else, officers sometimes harbor inappropriate attitudes and beliefs about victims. Check your attitudes against the following misconceptions.

Eight Myths about Victims

1. Abused women seek punishment.

This myth ignores economic, psychological, and social reality. A mistreated woman may lack the money, friends, confidence, or life skills to leave an abusive relationship. Many abusive men systematically destroy their mates' self-esteem, so that escape becomes difficult or impossible. When children are present, safety and financial issues may keep a woman from leaving. Of course the same dynamics may be seen when a woman abuses a male partner, and in homosexual relationships.

2. Men can't be expected to resist the charms of attractive women.

This myth, which unfairly makes women responsible for rapes and assaults, ignores a basic fact. These are crimes of power, not sex. The sexual freedom that characterizes contemporary life means that willing partners are readily available to men seeking sexual gratification. Rapists and other abusers are looking for something quite different: the experience of powering and humiliating a woman. A woman's age, appearance, clothing, and behavior are often irrelevant to a rapist.

3. If a woman submits, it can't be called rape.

This myth allows men to use any weapons at their disposal to force a woman's consent; it also blames the victim, not the rapist, for the crime. Aggression and force negate a woman's ability to say no. Fear can easily immobilize a woman; if the man is strong enough to assault her, a weapon may not even be necessary. Aggression can be verbal (threats against herself and others, for example) as well as physical.

4. Women secretly enjoy being hit and beaten.

5. Hitting and beating are normal events in most marriages and love relationships.

Both myths encourage abusers to solve problems through violence. These attitudes victimize women and children, destroy families, and fill up the trauma units in hospitals. (And men too can be victimized by this myth.) Domestic violence should always be taken seriously.

6. *Only minority and low-income families have trouble with domestic violence.*

This mistaken attitude may cause an officer to discount a complaint from a middle- or upper-income citizen. All complaints about violence (from children as well as adults) should be investigated, and offenders should always be prosecuted.

Avoid too the attitude that domestic violence is a fact of life in low-income areas. Some officers mistakenly believe that violence is permissible in certain neighborhoods. Every adult and child has the right to physical safety, regardless of lifestyle or income.

7. *If you are an officer, it is all right to ignore crimes against people you dislike.*

An anti-Semitic officer may not want to talk to a man who found swastikas painted on his front porch early this morning. A heterosexual officer may be uncomfortable dealing with a dispute between two gay men. Crimes in low-income areas are sometimes ignored by middle-income officers.

But conscientious officers treat all victims with respect, regardless of their feelings, for three reasons. First, the American justice system is built upon the principle of "liberty and justice for all." Second, law enforcement officers need support from the whole community, not just those they personally identify with and like. Third, social mobility is a fact of life in our culture. There is no sociological justification for assuming that one group of people is fundamentally different from another.

When citizens know you as a human being like themselves, and respect what you stand for, they are far more likely to cooperate with you and your agency. Everyone you meet has a network of friends and relatives who are likely to hear about your attitude and behavior. Courteous professionalism builds a reputation for trust and respect for you and your agency. Months or even years later, the image you have created may help you deal effectively with a dispute, a criminal investigation, or an outbreak of violence.

8. *All members of a minority group are alike.*

Most officers dislike being stereotyped, and citizens feel the same way about being lumped together. It is not true that all children, women, senior citizens, Jews, Catholics, Muslims, African Americans, Hispanics, Asian Americans, gays, or lesbians are alike. In your dealings with citizens, get to know them as individuals.

Encourage your agency to get involved in community activities involving all segments of the local population. While off-duty, seek opportunities to meet minorities who are law-abiding, responsible citizens.

Questions for Discussion

1. List the ethnic, religious, economic, and other groups in your community. Which groups enjoy the most prestige? The least? How might these factors affect an officer investigating a crime?

2. What emotions do you think you might experience when you investigate a crime? How might those emotions affect the victims with whom you are working?

Meeting the Needs of Victims

Crime victims have special needs. As a law enforcement officer, you have a unique opportunity to offer support in the critical moments when a crime is first reported. A few carefully chosen words can be a huge comfort to persons coping with a devastating experience. Follow these guidelines whenever you talk to a victim:

1. Be professional.

To a crime victim, you represent security, justice, and hope. Your calm competence can be a source of strength to the citizens you assist.

2. Minimize unnecessary questions.

Interviews are painful for victims. If others are investigating, coordinate your efforts so that victims do not face a succession of officers asking the same questions. Stifle your personal curiosity, and stick to the questions needed for a professional report. If you need a particular fact later on, check the official report instead of contacting the victim unnecessarily. Be especially sensitive with children. Repeated, unnecessary questions about physical or sexual abuse cause great suffering and accomplish little.

3. Do not blame.

Do not increase the victim's suffering by asking questions that suggest he or she caused the crime. Sometimes victims complain that they were questioned in such a hostile, suspicious manner that they felt like lawbreakers themselves. Don't criticize a rape victim because she is provocatively dressed, drank too much alcohol, or trusted the wrong man. Remember that rape is a crime of power, not sex. Similarly, don't criticize burglary victims who were careless with keys; don't tell accident victims they should have been more careful; don't ask an abused spouse why he or she didn't leave the relationship. Your job is to prosecute lawbreakers, not victims.

Take the time to reassure any children involved in the crime that they, too, are innocent. Because children think magically, not logically, they are likely to invent reasons to blame themselves. Children need to be reminded that they did not cause the incident and could not have prevented it. No child should feel responsible for protecting his or her parents or rescuing siblings from danger.

4. Listen patiently and compassionately.

In times of pain and fear, people need to express their feelings. Few words are necessary on your part. Your accepting presence can be the first step toward healing for a person who is suffering. During an interview, make sure the victim is seated in a safe, comfortable, and private place. Don't hurry the interview; impatience and insensitivity may increase the pain a victim is feeling. See Chapter 5 for other suggestions.

5. Reassure frightened victims.

Victims may need to be reminded that they are safe now. If their fear is still very strong, suggest they spend a few days away from the scene in the home of a friend or relative. Consider whether additional protection is needed, and take any steps necessary.

Some victims—especially those who were sexually attacked—may need encouragement to press charges. Assure them that they have nothing to be ashamed of, that they did not provoke the crime, and that your agency is eager to apprehend the criminal. Emphasize the importance of getting medical help and preventing further crimes.

Victims of domestic violence may need the same reassurance. Offenders often minimize the severity of their behavior; spouses and children may feel guilty about seeking help. Remind family members that spouse abuse and child abuse are never deserved, no matter how guilty victims may feel.

6. Recommend professional help when needed.

Victims may need outside help to deal with the aftereffects of a crime. A home or car that once seemed safe may now hold painful memories. Victims may have trouble shaking off their depression, fear, guilt, and anger to return to normal living. They need to know that it is normal to recover slowly (the process may take a year or more), and professional help is available—and recommended.

When support is lacking, the pain associated with a crime may destroy friendships and relationships. Illness, divorce, or even suicide may follow—tragedies that can be prevented with professional assistance.

7. *Offer appropriate information to the victim.*

Some officers resent victims' questions, feeling that police work should be protected by a veil of mystery. But victims need to feel that they are important participants in the justice process. They are entitled to courteous answers to their questions and clear, easy-to-understand explanations and police procedures. In addition, make sure that victims have appropriate referrals to community services that can offer medical, financial, and emotional support during times of crisis.

Questions for Discussion

1. How have attitudes toward women changed in the last 25 years? How have those changes affected investigations of crimes against women?

2. How have beliefs about children changed in the last 25 years? How have those changes affected investigations of crimes against children?

Summary

1. Victims are important people in the criminal justice system and should be treated with respect and courtesy.

2. Officers need to be aware of misconceptions that can cause unfair treatment of victims.

3. Avoid increasing victims' suffering through unnecessary questions, blaming, and shaming them about their experiences.

Multiple-Choice Questions

1. When dealing with a victim, officers should

   a) avoid discussions of police procedures.

b)   avoid blame.

c)   share the victim's feelings.

d)   all of the above.

2. The crime of rape

a)   can often be attributed to a woman's dress and behavior.

b)   requires cooperation from the woman.

c)   originates in the criminal's drive for power.

d)   all of the above.

3. When children are victims of crime,

a)   they often blame themselves for what happened.

b)   repeated interviews are necessary to help them separate fantasy from reality.

c)   the crime is unlikely to have long-lasting results.

d)   they need to learn responsibility for their behavior.

4. An officer investigating domestic violence should be aware that

a)   the definition of *domestic violence* may vary according to ethnic group, economic status, and local standards.

b)   some women deliberately provoke men to abuse them.

c)   both partners usually share responsibility for what happened.

d)   none of the above.

5. Crimes against homosexuals

a)   are not as serious as crimes against other citizens.

b)   should be thoroughly investigated.

c)   do not fall under the jurisdiction of most police agencies.

d)   none of the above.

CHAPTER EIGHT

PROBLEM SOLVING

Why Learn Problem-Solving Strategies?

As an officer you may spend a great deal of time negotiating agreements. Citizens often ask law enforcement agencies to settle disputes about money, property, and family life; you may also be involved in conflicts within the larger community, and within your agency itself.

Because conflict is a daily occurrence, we all need to develop problem-solving abilities. Your career in law enforcement demands an extra measure of those abilities, for you must often deal with the added dimensions of danger and fear. The problem-solving skills in this chapter (which can also be called "conflict resolution techniques") are equally useful in solving agency and family problems.

In many cases the arguers will have unsuccessfully tried to settle the dispute themselves before calling your agency. Threats, insults, and blows may be exchanged before your arrival. Each party will claim to be in the right and insist that you agree. You are responsible for protecting the parties, restoring order, following legal procedures, and—when appropriate—resolving the conflict. Do not, however, use negotiation or facilitation as an alternative to arresting a person who has committed a violent act. Remember too that your role does *not* include taking sides, moralizing, acting as a judge, or meting out punishment.

When a law has been broken, negotiation may be impossible. Arrests must be made, injured parties tended to, and evidence collected. At other times you may assist citizens to resolve a problem themselves.

Sometimes a neighborhood disagreement, rental problem, or consumer difficulty can be dealt with on the spot. Regardless of their age, income, education, or other factors, many citizens are capable of working out satisfactory solutions to problems. In some cases you may be involved in negotiations because no legal guidelines apply to the issue. If arguing neighbors have not broken a law, you may wish to use your own resources to settle the problem.

Questions for Discussion

1. Describe some of the problem-solving experiences you've had outside of law enforcement. What did you learn that you can apply to police work?

2. Recall a time when you solved a problem yourself instead of relying on an expert or authority figure to solve it for you. How did that experience turn out for you?

Problem-Solving Guidelines

Step One: Restoring Order

Always think first about protecting your own life and the lives and property of others. Use your powers of observation and the strategies you have been taught to ensure that no weapons—or objects that could be used as weapons—are within reach. Check for injuries, and seek medical help if necessary. Pay close attention to nonverbal messages. Disputants may assure you that there's no danger of violence, but their body language may tell you otherwise.

Put yourself in charge, limiting the movements and actions of the persons involved. If violence seems likely, consider separating them for the initial interview. If you are alone with an angry pair, consider calling for assistance. As you read in Chapter 4, you can avoid the complications of the rescue triangle by having four persons, rather than three, at the scene.

Avoid handling a dispute in front of bystanders. An onlooking audience can inflame a disagreement into life-threatening violence. If a couple is arguing, remove other family members from the immediate scene—or remove the couple themselves. On the other hand, you may decide that it is safe and beneficial to have the two parties listen silently to each other's side of the story. In a public dispute involving many people, try to choose one representative from each group, and take them aside so that no audience is listening.

Remain vigilant as you proceed to the next steps in settling the dispute. Even when the parties seem calm and reasonable, violence may erupt at any time.

Step Two: Listening

Bring the two parties together, and explain that you're there to help resolve the situation. Establish ground rules. You will not act as judge, although you may offer suggestions; each person will have a chance to talk without interruption; both parties will stay focused on the goal of resolving the problem; courtesy is required.

Remain neutral while you listen to each person's account of the conflict. Do not allow interruptions, and avoid interjecting your own opinion. Nod, make eye contact, and respond courteously to each speaker. Make sure both parties have a fair chance to be heard.

During this fact-finding step, intervene only when necessary—for example, to cut off name-calling, threats, or other inflammatory language. You might say something like this: "Mr. Brown, that kind of talk isn't going to get us anywhere. Will you agree to stick to the facts about what actually happened?"

Step Three: Facilitating an Agreement

When arguing parties are so at odds that a law enforcement agency must intervene, you might think there is little you can do to settle the dispute. Surprisingly often, however, an experienced officer can facilitate a workable agreement. Often the persons involved have been so focused on their own anger that they have failed to listen to the other side. If you can help them see each other's point of view, a compromise may suddenly seem desirable. The key principle is to avoid acting as a judge. Instead of imposing your opinion, allow citizens to work out their own solution, with your guidance.

Working out an Agreement

1. Do not attempt any negotiation until order has been restored.

Your first priorities are safety and order. Don't start thinking about solving the problem until you're sure that no one is in danger.

2. Refuse to take sides.

If you feel manipulated, say, "I'm here to help you resolve this problem, not to judge you. Can we get back to the issues?"

3. Focus your attention on outcomes rather than causes.

The past is over and cannot be changed. The parties can, however, make choices about their future behavior. Urge them to consider a proposal for ending the dispute now, before further damage is done:

> OFFICER: There's only a three-dollar difference between the restaurant bill and what Mr. Brown is willing to pay. Could you two split the difference and end the unpleasantness right now?

> MANAGER: Sounds good to me. I'm tired of arguing, and it's not getting us anywhere.

4. Make the parties aware of the disadvantages of stubbornness and the advantages of cooperation.

Describe the future they will face if they can't resolve their differences: continued tension, anger, and fear, along with the negative impact on customers, neighbors, children, and other family members.

5. Offer to educate the arguing parties.

For example, a frustrated landlord may not understand eviction procedures; arguing neighbors may not know that local ordinances regulate barking dogs, uncut grass, disabled vehicles, and similar problems.

6. Isolate negotiable issues and encourage disputants to work out appropriate settlements.

Use any information and life experience you have to make the settlement as attractive as possible:

OFFICER: A county ordinance says that dogs must be confined to the owner's property or under the owner's voice control. Miss White, what if Mrs. Clarkson agreed to obey this ordinance? Then she'd be able to keep Bowser for protection, and you wouldn't have to worry about your flowers being dug up any more. It seems to me that Bowser is good protection for you too, since he can see into your yard from his doghouse. My neighbor has a large dog, and I'm glad to have it living right next door.

MISS WHITE: I never thought of that before. Bowser always barks when he hears something suspicious late at night.

MRS. CLARKSON: I guess I can keep Bowser inside my fence, if that's what the county wants me to do.

7. When you are negotiating a solution, begin with a small issue and gradually work up to larger ones.

Foster a sense of agreement and cooperation between both parties before you ask them to tackle a large problem.

8. After a solution has been reached, ask for a commitment from both parties.

Do not assume that a solution you like is going to please everyone. Not all disputes can—or should—be settled on the spot by an officer. But every problem solved by the parties themselves, with your help, makes your community a better place and lessens the burdens on the legal system. Keep developing your negotiating skills. They will reward your efforts again and again.

Questions for Discussion

1. What factors might guide an officer who is unsure about trying to facilitate an agreement in a particular problem?

2. Sometimes facilitation is a slower process than an arrest. What are the advantages to the participants, the community, and your agency when you take the time to do a successful facilitation?

Summary

1. Safety is the first issue to be considered in problem-solving negotiations.

2. Life experience, legal knowledge, and communication skills are important aids in the facilitation process.

3. The officer's role is to protect the parties and their property, to listen impartially, and to help the parties focus on the central issues in the dispute.

Multiple-Choice Questions

1. When an officer is called to handle a problem, the first priority should be

   a) deciding whether to make an arrest or facilitate an agreement.

   b) hearing the facts.

   c) protecting everyone's safety.

   d) separating the arguing parties.

2. Facilitation should be ruled out unless

   a) both parties are longtime friends.

   b) the officer already knows who's at fault.

   c) no legal guidelines apply to the problem.

   d) an agreement seems workable.

3. During a facilitation, an officer should

   a) keep the parties focused on the present and future, not the past.

   b) encourage both parties to acknowledge their past mistakes.

   c) encourage participation from others involved in the incident.

   d) prevent each party from hearing the other person's version of the incident in question.

4. When disputing parties negotiate their own solution to their problems,

   a) the police officer loses prestige.

   b) compliance is unlikely.

   c) the risk of violence increases.

   d) the criminal justice system saves time and money.

5. During a facilitation, an officer may

   a) act as judge.

   b) use threats to hasten the process.

   c) ask onlookers for their opinions.

   d) educate the parties about ordinances and laws.

CHAPTER NINE

SEXUAL HARASSMENT ISSUES

The Problem of Sexual Harassment

Because law enforcement is traditionally masculine, female officers have sometimes been expected to adopt a tolerant "boys will be boys" attitude toward off-color jokes, profanity, and sexual pictures, cartoons, and calendars. But as our society becomes more sensitive to sexual harassment, officers are being held to stricter standards. Officers need to be well informed about the legal risks associated with sexual harassment, which can be defined as "deliberate and/or repeated sexual or sex-based behavior that is not welcome, not asked for, and not returned."

Sexual harassment can be verbal or nonverbal, and both men and women can be victimized. Most often, however, the harasser is male and the victim is female. Any unwelcome attention or touching—no matter what the intent—may fall into the category of sexual harassment.

Like sexual battery, sexual harassment is usually about power, not sex. Because a victim's livelihood can be at risk, workplaces are charged with the responsibility to create a safe and nonthreatening workplace. Subjecting a person to a hostile working environment can lead to serious charges and even dismissal from a job.

Because individuals vary in their tolerance of sexual innuendo, it can sometimes be difficult to differentiate between acceptable and nonacceptable behavior. The best practice, therefore, is to avoid any behavior that might be misconstrued—and to stop immediately when asked to. Repeated, unwelcome behavior—even if it was intended to flatter or amuse—may be labeled harassment. Penalties can be severe.

Equal Employment Opportunity Commission (EEOC) guidelines say that employers must prevent sexual harassment from occurring. If it does occur, immediate and appropriate action must be taken to correct it. Supervisors are legally required to assist anyone who complains about the following:

> feeling uncomfortable working in a sexually charged atmosphere (sexual pictures, cartoons, calendars, jokes)
>
> being addressed sexually, not professionally ("Honey," "Cutie," "Legs")
>
> coping with unwanted attention (love letters, poems, notes, telephone calls, repeated requests for dates)
>
> being touched inappropriately (caressed, patted, pinched, kissed, grabbed)
>
> being plagued by intimate questions about his or her body, clothing, or personal life
>
> being spoken of as sexually needy, deprived, or confused

Questions for Discussion

1. What characteristics of police work create particular challenges to agencies committed to prohibiting sexual harassment?

2. How could charges of sexual harassment affect an officer's career?

3. What positive steps might an agency take to ensure female employees and citizens a nonthreatening environment?

Creating a Positive Working Environment

Sometimes agencies are reluctant to confront officers about sexually suggestive behavior that has long been tolerated. Be aware, however, that sexual harassment endangers everyone—both male and female—in an agency. Morale, loyalty, and teamwork always suffer when men and women are hostile to one another. A belittling attitude toward women creates mistrust and anger, and it can damage your agency's relationship to the larger community. Visitors to your agency should never be confronted with offensive visual material—for example, cartoons, signs, or calendars that demean women. Jokes about rape and spouse abuse should not be tolerated in an agency charged with the protection of citizens, both male and female. As an officer, make it a priority to ensure that women both inside and outside your agency are treated with respect.

Questions for Discussion

1. How can an agency show that it respects its female officers?

2. What undesirable consequences—aside from the possibility of legal penalties—might cause an agency to adopt a no-tolerance policy about sexual harassment?

Summary

1. Sexual harassment can be defined as "deliberate and/or repeated sexual or sex-based behavior that is not welcome, not asked for, and not returned."

2. Supervisors can be held responsible for employees' harassing behavior.

3. A humorous or teasing intent does not justify sexual harassment.

Multiple-Choice Questions

1. Which of the following might be labeled a form of sexual harassment?

    a) a compliment about a woman's legs.

    b) a provocative picture on a calendar in an office.

    c) a joke about rape.

    d) all of these.

2. Police agencies traditionally have

    a) been overcautious in their treatment of female officers.

    b) expected female officers to tolerate sexual humor.

    c) encouraged women to file harassment charges.

    d) none of these.

3. An attractive female officer often hears admiring comments from male officers. She has asked the men to stop commenting on her appearance. She

    a) should thank them graciously for the compliments.

    b) should consider another career.

    c) can file harassment charges.

    d) should consider psychological counseling.

4. Nonverbal sexual attention on the job is

    a) potentially a form of sexual harassment.

    b) normal when men and women work long hours together.

    c) acceptable as long as there is no physical contact.

    d) acceptable if the woman receiving the attention is not married.

5. Sexual teasing and jokes are

   a) a normal part of modern working life.

   b) often used to demean women.

   c) trivial, everyday occurrences.

   d) acceptable if they are truly funny.

CHAPTER TEN

MONITORING YOUR ATTITUDE

A Positive Attitude

Monitoring your attitude each day is one of the best ways to communicate effectively. The ability to maintain a positive outlook despite the ups and downs of life and work will do much to help you maintain good relationships with the important people in your life.

It is likely that you chose a criminal justice career because you want to make a significant contribution to society. That desire can keep you motivated during discouraging moments—but it also makes you a candidate for stress and burnout. Keep your motivation high by focusing on the present moment. Give yourself credit for each small accomplishment, and take pride in performing routine tasks well. Remember that an incident that seems minor to you may be remembered for a long time by the citizens you deal with. Years after a brief encounter with an officer, many citizens continue to be grateful for a small extra effort or additional courtesy. Take pride in each opportunity to be a positive force in your community.

Telling the Truth

Honesty is the first principle taught in 12-step programs, and it's an effective communication tool as well. Besides helping your mind and body deal more effectively with stress, it builds bonds with other people, both on and off the job.

Do not deny facts and feelings. Don't smother them with food, drown them in alcohol, project them onto your family or fellow of-

68

ficers, or blast them away with macho street talk. Allow yourself to acknowledge the inevitable fears and frustrations of your job. Develop relationships with others who deal honestly with their feelings. "Stress debriefings" can be lifesaving.

Avoid the "John Wayne syndrome"—pretending you're a lone crusader for justice, untroubled by doubts or fears. Modern law enforcement is less concerned with toughness than it used to be. There is much more emphasis on problem solving, communication, and sensitivity. Don't be afraid to face your emotions honestly.

Spend a few minutes talking over each day's events with a trusted friend before you return home. Look for someone with a high level of commitment to law enforcement. A cynical officer may increase your stress level instead of easing it.

When negative feelings are defused this way, they don't have a chance to build up. But when negative feelings are denied, they turn into monsters whose destructive power can ruin your health, family life, and career.

Honest talk with other officers can empower you to work for needed changes in law enforcement. If you're frustrated by the constraints you face in carrying out your duties, seek power in numbers. Get involved in a professional organization, and work with other officers for change.

Get Involved with the Larger World

An important strategy for maintaining a positive attitude is to forge strong connections with the larger world outside law enforcement. The criminal justice field often focuses on people at their worst. If you spend most of your time with lawbreakers and officers, you may rapidly lose your perspective. Good alternatives include family time, health clubs, community organizations, church activities, and socializing with friends in other professions. Resist the "I don't have time" excuse. Exploring new ways to spend your leisure time will benefit you much more than sitting in front of the TV—or in a lounge. Your morale will improve, you'll win friends for your agency, and you'll be sharing your gifts and knowledge with an ever-widening circle of people.

Maintaining Your Perspective

If you have been involved in law enforcement for several years, you may have noticed negative changes in some of the officers you know. Often the deterioration is slow and gradual—the result of a buildup of small annoyances. Try to eliminate some of the daily irritants that cause headaches and frayed tempers. For example, don't allow yourself to be overwhelmed by minor tasks during your time off—unless you truly enjoy puttering around the house. Alternatives include delegating jobs to other family members, hiring someone else to do them, or simplifying your lifestyle to minimize home and automobile maintenance. Schedule a family meeting to plan strategies that will make your time off more enjoyable. To ensure that the meeting will be positive and productive, assure your spouse and children that you're concerned about their stress levels too.

Make a realistic assessment of yourself, your time, and your abilities. Don't burden yourself by expecting to do the impossible, and don't berate yourself for mistakes. Many idealists increase their stress by clinging to overblown expectations of themselves.

Remind yourself often that your career allows you to reach out to people in need during the critical moments in their lives. Your words and gestures can have a lasting effect on those around you. Never underestimate the importance of what you are doing. Frequently remind yourself that you are providing a vital service to your community.

Enriching Your Life

Research suggests that one of the best weapons against negativism is an activity you do regularly for enjoyment. You will know you have found the right activity if you lose track of time when you're focused on doing it.

Unfortunately, many people talk themselves out of activities they enjoy because they feel tired and drained after working. The result is increased fatigue, boredom, depression, and emptiness. Missed opportunities for fun can lead to a rapid deterioration in a love relationship. You are at high risk for disease or divorce if your life gives you nothing to look forward to but a glass of liquor at the end of your shift.

Recreation—preferably with family and friends outside of law enforcement—is not a luxury. It's a necessity for anyone who works hard. Clear a space for your favorite activities, and enjoy them as much as you can. They are true lifesavers.

Questions for Discussion

1. Why might officers be tempted not to "tell the truth" about their own stress factors?

2. What communication skills might encourage officers to "tell the truth"?

3. Why might some officers lose contact with the world outside of law enforcement?

Summary

1. Honest communication with trusted friends can help officers maintain a positive attitude.

2. Small irritants can gradually erode an officer's morale and effectiveness.

3. Recreation is vital to physical health and personal relationships.

Multiple-Choice Questions

1. The "John Wayne" syndrome can cause an officer to

   a) watch late-night television excessively.

   b) fantasize about the Old West instead of dealing with contemporary problems.

   c) lose touch with the realities of police work today.

   d) brag endlessly about past encounters with lawbreakers.

2. Minor irritants

   a) can gradually cause an officer's attitude to deteriorate.

   b) do not cause problems for dedicated officers.

   c) usually disappear if they're ignored.

   d) are rare in law enforcement work.

3. Friendships with fellow officers

   a) are more important than friendships outside of law enforcement.

   b) distract officers from their responsibilities.

   c) need to be balanced with other relationships.

   d) all of the above.

4. Activities outside of law enforcement
   a) should be discouraged for officers.
   b) are permissible if time permits.
   c) are permissible for unmarried officers.
   d) can help officers maintain a positive attitude toward their work.

5. Reminding yourself often that you are helping your community
   a) can help you maintain a positive attitude.
   b) can damage agency morale if you work with some cynical officers.
   c) will make you pompous and self-righteous.
   d) is an example of the "John Wayne" syndrome.

ADDITIONAL QUESTIONS FOR DISCUSSION

1. Think of an authority figure who made a positive impression on you when you were growing up—and one who made a negative impression. Compare and contrast them. What did you learn by observing them? How can you apply that knowledge to your career?

2. Recall a time when you sought help from an authority figure and were turned down. What were your feelings? How do you wish the situation had been handled? What principles do you plan to follow when you are asked for help on the job?

3. Have you ever been put into an uncomfortable or dangerous situation because of something your partner or coworker said? How did you handle the situation?

4. Describe an incident in which you played one or more "rescue triangle" roles. How could the situation have been handled more productively?

5. Describe a person you have known who often has assumed one of the rescue triangle roles. (Be careful to protect the person's privacy.) Then list several strategies for dealing effectively with that person.

6. Recall a time when you were interviewed in connection with school, work, or some other situation. What feelings did you experience? Did the interviewer help to put you at ease—or make the interview difficult for you? How would you evaluate the listening skills of this interviewer?

7. Describe a person in your family or circle of friends who has special needs (illness, a member of a minority group, a disability, or some other factor). What guidelines do you follow when

you spend time with that person? Which of those guidelines might be helpful in your dealings with citizens who have special needs?

8. List as many reasons as you can why people are sometimes insensitive. Then list a remedy for as many of those reasons as you can.

9. Recall a time when you felt mistreated. List the emotions you remember feeling at the time. How did those emotions affect your thinking and behavior? How might they affect a crime victim trying to cooperate with a police investigation?

10. Describe someone well known to you whom you consider a good problem solver. What exceptional qualities does that person have that you can emulate?

SCENARIOS

A note to instructors: These scenarios can be used for classroom discussion and role-playing as well as written assignments.

Scenario #1

You are investigating a daytime burglary. The homeowner tells you that the woman who lives next door is home all day and may have seen the intruder. When you go to the house, a little girl tells you that her grandmother speaks very little English. Both the child and grandmother seem fearful about talking to you. How will you handle this situation?_____

_____

_____

_____

_____

_____

_____

_____

_____

_____

_____

_____

_____

Scenario #2

You are investigating a traffic accident. One driver is an elderly man whose speech indicates he may have had little formal education. You ask, "Do you have a preference as to the wrecker service that will tow your car from the accident scene?" He says he does not understand you. Then you ask, "Who do you want to tow your car?" He tells you the name of a wrecker service. What communication principles will help you in a similar situation in the future? _____

_____

_____

_____

_____

_____

_____

_____

_____

_____

_____

_____

_____

_____

_____

_____

_____

Scenario #3

You are conducting a rape investigation. The victim is fearful and very reluctant to talk about what happened. She appears to distrust law enforcement, especially male officers. How will you handle this situation? _____

_____

_____

_____

_____

_____

_____

_____

_____

_____

_____

_____

_____

_____

_____

_____

_____

Scenario #4

You arrive at the scene of a domestic violence call. You hear a man and a woman yelling at each other. You see the man ball up his fist and draw his arm back as if he is going to strike the woman. How will you handle this situation?_____

_____

_____

_____

_____

_____

_____

_____

_____

_____

_____

_____

_____

_____

_____

_____

_____

_____

Scenario #5

You are investigating an argument between a husband and a wife. The husband, who has left the house already, destroyed the living-room furniture. You explain to the wife that there is nothing you can do because the furniture is as much his as hers. He has the right to destroy his own property. How do you think this makes the victim feel about law enforcement? What communication principles could help you improve her perception of law enforcement?

_____

_____

_____

_____

_____

_____

_____

_____

_____

_____

_____

_____

_____

_____

_____

Scenario #6

You are attempting to arrest an intoxicated individual who is causing a disturbance in a local bar. He calls you by another officer's name and threatens to "kick your ass" because "you gave me a speeding ticket." You have never encountered this person before. How will you handle this situation?_____

_____

_____

_____

_____

_____

_____

_____

_____

_____

_____

_____

_____

_____

_____

_____

Scenario #7

You are a white officer assigned to investigate a theft in a predominantly black neighborhood. You talk to the complainant, an elderly black woman, who immediately demands to speak to a black officer because "you white people won't help us black folks." How will you handle this situation? _____

_____

_____

_____

_____

_____

_____

_____

_____

_____

_____

_____

_____

_____

_____

_____

Scenario #8

You are a backup officer on a traffic stop. The driver, a 16-year-old girl, hands you her driver's license and registration. You overhear the other officer say, "You stupid blondes are all the same. The next time I stop you, I will take you to jail!" How would you deal with the driver? The other officer? _____

_____

_____

_____

_____

_____

_____

_____

_____

_____

_____

_____

_____

_____

_____

_____

Scenario #9

You have been called to a crash and are investigating the driver for suspicion of driving under the influence. Many years ago, your mother was seriously injured in a traffic accident. You begin to taunt the driver in hopes that he will make some gesture that would justify your using force against him to effect the arrest. What consequences might follow? _____

_____

_____

_____

_____

_____

_____

_____

_____

_____

_____

_____

_____

_____

_____

Scenario #10

You and your partner are investigating a domestic dispute. Your partner is questioning the woman, who is crying hysterically and saying that the man grabbed her and pushed her down. You are questioning the man, who tells you "She only gets this way when she drinks." He insists that he grabbed her by the arm to keep her from falling and injuring herself. He says, "You know how emotional women are, Officer." How will you handle this situation? _____

_____

_____

_____

_____

_____

_____

_____

_____

_____

_____

_____

_____

_____

_____

_____

_____

Scenario #11

You and another officer are on patrol when you see a driver traveling approximately 70 mph in a 45 mph zone. You pull the vehicle over, and your partner exits the patrol vehicle first. You see that the driver is a juvenile male. Your partner pulls his service weapon and orders the driver to exit his vehicle with his hands up. The driver complies. Your partner then orders the juvenile to face the car and place his hands on the vehicle. The juvenile complies. You then see your partner begin to strike the juvenile with his fists in the ribs. What would you do? _____

_____

_____

_____

_____

_____

_____

_____

_____

_____

_____

_____

_____

_____

Scenario #12

You and another officer are working a security detail at a local high school football game. Your partner sees a black male juvenile walking toward you. Your partner shouts, "Hey, Boy, get over here. I want to talk to you." The juvenile shouts back, "Don't call me boy!" Your partner shouts back, "I'll call you whatever I want to" and pushes him. How would you handle the officer in this situation? The juvenile?_____

_____

_____

_____

_____

_____

_____

_____

_____

_____

_____

_____

_____

_____

_____

_____

Scenario #13

You are at a private home attempting to arrest a man for violation of probation. When he answers the door, you tell him that he is under arrest. He asks to change his shirt because the one he's wearing is dirty. You allow him to go to his bedroom by himself because you don't want to embarrass him in front of his children. What communication skills should you use to maintain control? _____

_____

_____

_____

_____

_____

_____

_____

_____

_____

_____

_____

_____

_____

_____

Scenario #14

You are investigating a shoplifting at a local department store. The store manager takes you to the office where the suspect is being detained. You recognize the suspect as a city council member. She is insisting that she be released because she didn't take anything. She says, "Don't you all know who I am?" and threatens to have your badge if you arrest her. How will you handle this situation?_____

_____

_____

_____

_____

_____

_____

_____

_____

_____

_____

_____

_____

_____

_____

_____

_____

Scenario #15

You are dispatched to a house to handle a domestic disturbance. When you arrive, you see that the woman has a cut lip, and her right eye is red and swollen. The man is irate and insists that nothing is wrong. The woman will not talk to you at all. You tell the man that he is under arrest for domestic battery. What "rescuer behaviors" might the woman exhibit? _____

_____

_____

_____

_____

_____

_____

_____

_____

_____

_____

_____

_____

_____

_____

_____

_____

_____

Scenario #16

You are dispatched to a neighborhood disturbance. You see two Hispanic men arguing loudly in the middle of the street. You are not Hispanic. You try to separate the men and restore order. Both men tell you that you have no business in their neighborhood, and that they will settle the problem themselves. How will you handle this situation?

_____

_____

_____

_____

_____

_____

_____

_____

_____

_____

_____

_____

_____

_____

_____

_____

Scenario #17

You stop a driver for speeding after investigating a traffic crash where a young child on a bicycle was seriously injured by a speeding driver. You begin berating the driver about his irresponsible driving. What role are you assuming, and how can you better deal with this situation?____

_____

_____

_____

_____

_____

_____

_____

_____

_____

_____

_____

_____

_____

_____

_____

Scenario #18

You are a trainee assigned to a veteran officer. He has told you to sit in the squad car, say nothing, ask no questions, and do exactly what he does when handling calls. He tells you that you can forget what you learned in the academy because you are now in the "real world." To complete your field training successfully, you must do exactly what he says. What role is he exhibiting? How can you deal effectively with this situation? _____

_____

_____

_____

_____

_____

_____

_____

_____

_____

_____

_____

_____

_____

_____

_____

Scenario #19

You arrest a juvenile for shoplifting. He calls you a "Honky Cracker" and declares that you arrested him solely because he's black. What is he trying to do? What actions can you take to avoid escalating the confrontation?

_____

_____

_____

_____

_____

_____

_____

_____

_____

_____

_____

_____

_____

_____

_____

Scenario #20

While on patrol, you see a woman who is having difficulty with her balance as she walks down the street. You talk to her to find out what is wrong. Her speech is slurred, but you don't smell liquor. She shows you identification. You realize she probably has cerebral palsy. What skills would be useful in communicating with her? _____

_____

_____

_____

_____

_____

_____

_____

_____

_____

_____

_____

_____

_____

_____

_____

_____

Scenario #21

You are a male officer. Late one night you are dispatched to the emergency room of the hospital to interview a rape victim. No female officer is available. What principles will guide you?_____

_____

_____

_____

_____

_____

_____

_____

_____

_____

_____

_____

_____

_____

_____

_____

_____

_____

Scenario #22

You are interviewing an elderly woman who is the victim of a theft. She tells you that someone stole a prized plant from her porch. She tells you the history of the plant, which leads into a discussion about the history of her family. What techniques would you use to keep the interview focused on the theft?_____

_____

_____

_____

_____

_____

_____

_____

_____

_____

_____

_____

_____

_____

_____

_____

_____

Scenario #23

It is Saturday morning, and the police department is closed for regular business. The main doors are locked, but citizens can use a ring-down phone beside them. A sign lists instructions for contacting the communications center after hours and on weekends and holidays. You are walking through the parking lot when a citizen approaches. The citizen asks you how to contact someone inside the department. You respond, "All you have to do is read the instructions on the front door." The citizen responds, "Officer, I can't read." What presumptions had you made? How did your attitude affect the citizen? The reputation of your agency? _____

_____

_____

_____

_____

_____

_____

_____

_____

_____

_____

_____

_____

_____

Scenario #24

You are at a private home, investigating a domestic dispute. The woman invites you in and begins to tell you what happened. Her husband enters the room, stands in front of her, and starts telling you what happened. How can you show sensitivity while maintaining control of the situation? ___

_____

_____

_____

_____

_____

_____

_____

_____

_____

_____

_____

_____

_____

_____

_____

_____

_____

Scenario #25

Rumors have started to circulate about an officer your agency hired two months ago. She is reputed to be a lesbian. Some other officers you have worked with for years are expecting you to join in their jokes and offensive remarks about her. How will you handle this situation? ___

_____

_____

_____

_____

_____

_____

_____

_____

_____

_____

_____

_____

_____

_____

_____

_____

Scenario #26

In the last five years, the demographics in your community have changed so that there is a much larger minority population. An African American mother calls your agency to complain that white teenaged boys in her neighborhood are taunting and throwing small objects at her. How do you handle this situation?_____

_____

_____

_____

_____

_____

_____

_____

_____

_____

_____

_____

_____

_____

_____

_____

_____

_____

Scenario #27

You meet with a couple whose home was burglarized. What communication skills could you use to help the victims deal not only with their property loss (jewelry and electronic equipment), but also the loss of their sense of security? _____

_____

_____

_____

_____

_____

_____

_____

_____

_____

_____

_____

_____

_____

_____

_____

Scenario #28

You are dispatched to a house where a man is threatening to commit suicide. When you knock on the door and identify yourself, you hear a male voice telling you to come in. You walk into the living room and see a man sitting on a couch, holding a .38 revolver in his hand. He says he doesn't want to live anymore. How will you handle this situation?_____

_____

_____

_____

_____

_____

_____

_____

_____

_____

_____

_____

_____

_____

_____

_____

_____

Scenario #29

You go to a home to investigate a burglary. The man who answers the door begins waving his hands and making excited noises. You realize that he is deaf. No interpreter is nearby. How will you handle this situation? _____

_____

_____

_____

_____

_____

_____

_____

_____

_____

_____

_____

_____

_____

_____

_____

Scenario #30

You are dispatched to a downtown intersection to investigate a suspicious person. You locate an elderly woman dressed in a nightgown. She tells you her name, but she is disoriented and can't tell you where she lives. How will you handle this situation? _____

_____

_____

_____

_____

_____

_____

_____

_____

_____

_____

_____

_____

_____

_____

_____

_____

_____

_____

Scenario #31

A woman in her early twenties comes to headquarters to complain about a stalker. You learn that she has complained twice before, but nothing was done to help her. She says the officer she talked to before seemed amused about her plight and said, "Attractive women should expect to get lots of attention from lovesick men." What do you say to her? _____

_____

_____

_____

_____

_____

_____

_____

_____

_____

_____

_____

_____

_____

_____

Scenario #32

You and your partner are investigating a theft at a convenience store run by a family from Pakistan. While en route, your partner complains at length about foreigners who are taking jobs away from Americans. When you arrive, you talk to a clerk whose English is poor. Your partner interrupts with, "It would make our job easier if you would learn to speak English—or just go back where you came from." How would you handle the investigation?_____

_____

_____

_____

_____

_____

_____

_____

_____

_____

_____

_____

_____

_____

_____

_____

_____

Scenario #33

You are dispatched to a neighborhood dispute. Two neighbors are arguing about a privacy fence. One man tells you that the fence has been illegally erected on two feet of his property. What negotiation techniques could you use that would allow the neighbors to work out their own solution?

_____

_____

_____

_____

_____

_____

_____

_____

_____

_____

_____

_____

_____

_____

_____

_____

Scenario #34

You are the guest speaker at a Neighborhood Watch meeting. The members are concerned about a vacant lot that has become a gathering place for young adults at night. The neighbors are complaining about loud radios, litter, and offensive language late at night. How would you facilitate a solution? _____

_____

_____

_____

_____

_____

_____

_____

_____

_____

_____

_____

_____

_____

_____

_____

Scenario #35

You are called to handle a domestic dispute between a wife with an alcohol problem and her nondrinking, tough-talking husband. What factors will help you determine whether you should make an arrest or help the couple settle their problems?_____

_____

_____

_____

_____

_____

_____

_____

_____

_____

_____

_____

_____

_____

_____

_____

Scenario #36

You are dispatched to a downtown intersection, where two men are arguing about a dented fender. A crowd has gathered. Neither man seems interested in fighting the other. What steps will you take to restore order? _____

_____

_____

_____

_____

_____

_____

_____

_____

_____

_____

_____

_____

_____

_____

_____

_____

_____

Scenario #37

You are called to a church youth center. Two teenaged boys are fighting over a girl they claim to be in love with. The girl, looking terrified, is sitting in the youth director's office. Her parents are on their way to pick her up. How will you handle this situation? _____

_____

_____

_____

_____

_____

_____

_____

_____

_____

_____

_____

_____

_____

_____

_____

_____

Scenario #38

You are a patrol sergeant. A female officer under your supervision tells you that she is concerned about a fellow officer's inappropriate touching. Every time this officer talks to her, he puts his hand on her back, touches her arm, or touches her in another way she finds annoying. How will you handle this situation? _____

_____

_____

_____

_____

_____

_____

_____

_____

_____

_____

_____

_____

_____

_____

_____

_____

_____

_____

Scenario #39

You are a female patrol officer. You overhear a group of male officers in the hallway discussing female officers. One says, "Female officers are nothing but bitches and don't belong on the road." How will you handle this situation?_____

_____

_____

_____

_____

_____

_____

_____

_____

_____

_____

_____

_____

_____

_____

Scenario #40

An officer with years of experience objects to his agency's no-tolerance policy about sexual harassment. He complains that women are "taking over" and that the agency is "going soft." How will you handle this situation? _____

_____

_____

_____

_____

_____

_____

_____

_____

_____

_____

_____

_____

_____

_____

_____

_____

_____

_____

ANSWERS TO MULTIPLE-CHOICE QUESTIONS

Chapter One
Introduction to Communication

1. c
2. b
3. a
4. d
5. b

Chapter Two
Communicating Authority

1. d
2. b
3. a
4. a
5. c

Chapter Three
Dealing with Manipulation

1. a
2. d
3. b
4. c
5. b

Chapter Four
The Rescue Triangle

1. b
2. c
3. d
4. a
5. c

Chapter Five
Listening and Interviewing Skills

1. a
2. d
3. c
4. b
5. b

Chapter Six
Sensitivity

1. c
2. a
3. b
4. d
5. c

Chapter Seven
Crime Victims

1. b
2. c
3. a
4. d
5. b

Chapter Eight
Problem Solving

1. c
2. d
3. a
4. d
5. d

Chapter Nine
Sexual Harassment Issues

1. d
2. b
3. c
4. a
5. b

Chapter Ten
Monitoring Your Attitude

1. c
2. a
3. c
4. d
5. a